Lee Canter's

Parents
On Your Side®

Resource Materials Workbook

A Publication of Canter & Associates

Writer: Patricia Ryan Sarka
Editorial Staff: Marcia Shank, Kathy Winberry, Marlene Canter
Design: The Arcane Corporation
Illustrators: Jane Yamada and Patty Briles

©1991 Canter & Associates, Inc.
P.O. Box 66926, Los Angeles, CA 90066-6926
800-262-4347   310-578-4700
www.canter.net

ISBN #0-939007-40-1

Printed in the United States of America
First printing June 1991
04 03 02   13 12 11 10

PD4067

Table of Contents

Overview

Parents On Your Side

Teachers today are facing many obstacles to success in their classrooms. More and more students are coming to school with academic, behavior and motivation problems. These problems are often magnified, and more difficult to solve, because of a lack of parent support. This isn't a regional or economic problem: It faces every teacher, in every classroom throughout the nation.

Why is parent support so important? Parents are the most important people in a child's life. They provide a child's fundamental needs: love, affection support and approval. Because parents are #1 in importance in a child's life, they are also #1 in the ability to influence and motivate their children. As a teacher, you need their influence and motivation to help students overcome academic, behavior and motivation problems. With "parents on your side," the road to success is a much easier climb for everyone on the educational ladder—students, parents, and the teacher!

Parents today are a diverse group—single mothers, single fathers, stepmothers, stepfathers, newly arrived immigrants, the affluent, the middle class, and an ever-increasing number of poverty-level parents. Many of these are parents of "at risk" children. They want to help but they don't know how. Getting these parents involved is paramount to the success of your educational program.

Parents on Your Side is a step-by-step program developed to give teachers the skills needed to work effectively with today's parents. You will learn how to communicate effectively with parents by developing the skills and confidence necessary to get all parents to support your academic, discipline and homework efforts.

This *Parents on Your Side Resource Materials Workbook* is the perfect complement to the *Parents on Your Side* textbook (2nd ed.) and program. In this guide you will be given hands-on materials that correspond exactly with the text so that you can begin to implement your parent involvement program right now.

Lee Canter's
Parents
on your side

A Teacher's Guide to Creating Positive Relationships with Parents
2nd Edition

LEE CANTER AND MARLENE CANTER

Developing a Parent Involvement Plan for the Entire School Year

The most effective teachers get parents on their side even before school begins and continue positive, open communications with parents throughout the entire school year. These teachers know that when parents are involved their students do better academically and behaviorally. A kind word, an approving gesture, some one-on-one personal attention and help: these are powerful tools that parents need only be made aware of to insure a more successful school year for their children. And what parents want most for their children is success. Together with these parents, you can be the driving force behind a successful school year.

Before school begins, you need to develop a parent-involvement plan for the entire year. When your first interaction with parents is a positive one, you set a tone of cooperation and goodwill that will last throughout the year. The key to successful interaction with parents is your genuine concern for their child. From the start, look for occasions that will show your interest and concern. Notes home, phone calls, birthday greetings and get-well cards demonstrate to parents that your commitment to their child is genuine.

Regularly scheduled conferences can be perfect opportunities to encourage teamwork and get the support that will turn parents into partners. Use conferences to get parent input and to share concerns about their children. The way you plan for conferences (from gathering samples of student work to showing documentation of both positives and problems) is almost as important as how you conduct the conference, but the way you communicate or "how you say it" is more important than everything else.

Not all of your interaction with parents will be motivated by something positive the child has done. Problems with behavior or homework may initiate contact with parents. If you have laid a foundation of concern and trust with the parent and if you show confidence that the problem can be solved together—even this type of interaction can be positive. You can make these interactions positive by planning how you will communicate these problems to parents and just exactly what you will say. Planning gives you the confidence to demonstrate your professionalism to parents and lets them know you are confident of a solution to the problem.

Learning the procedures to deal effectively with parents in even the most difficult situations, on the phone or in person, is a most important skill. Early detection of problems and consulting parents when these problems first arise will stop many problems before they become serious. Prevention of problems is always preferable to curing them.

Specific parent-involvement plans, conference techniques, behavior and homework contracts and a variety of communication ideas that will foster positive parent support are included in this resource guide. For a more in-depth guide to gaining parent support, read the comprehensive text *Parents On Your Side*. It details how a teacher can gain parent support by understanding the roadblocks that both teachers and parents have that impede open communications.

How to Use This Book

The *Parents On Your Side Resource Materials Workbook* is divided into seven sections. These sections are arranged chronologically, throughout the school year. Each section gives you step-by-step instructions for achieving specific parent involvement goals. These instructions are followed by reproducibles, classroom aids, organizational ideas, motivators, charts and checklists that will enable you to have the most successful school year ever.

Let's all team up for a great school year!

Opening the Lines of Communication Before School Begins

First impressions are lasting impressions. Why not take the initiative to make positive contact with your new students and their parents before school begins? Don't be an unknown quantity the first day of school. Say "hello" by phone or letter. Your greeting need not be long or involved–just a caring teacher taking the time to say "hi" to new students and parents and to let them know that you're enthusiastic about the upcoming school year.

Welcoming Notes to Parents and Students

Use these letterheads (pages 9 and 10) to send your welcoming message. These brief notes are the building blocks for positive communications throughout the school year. You may wish to include the following information:

- Your full name
- School name, address, phone number
- Room number
- Date and time of first day of school
- Invitation to stop by and say "hi" on the first day (or anytime at the beginning of the school year)

Fold-a-Note Greetings

This is a perfect way to send a personal greeting. Reproduce, cut along the dotted line and you've got two note cards–ready for your back-to-school greeting. Just staple shut, address, stamp and mail. These notes (pages 11 and 12) can also be reproduced on colorful paper or index-card stock.

Student Postcards. . .

Postcards are the fastest and easiest way to get your positive message across. Printed four per page, these notes (see page 13) are ready to be personalized by you. Before you reproduce the postcard, write all pertinent information on the back: first day of school, time school or class begins, room number and your name. Then reproduce enough cards for each student in your class. Print on colorful index card stock. Cut them out and mail.

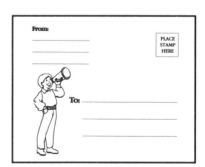

Note: Junior and high school teachers may choose to create a postcard message that specifically fits their needs–class title and time, room number, first-day supplies, etc. In that case, just reproduce the fronts of the postcards (page 12) and write your own personal message before you reproduce the cards.

Welcome Students

Welcome Parents

To:

_____

_____

_____

_____

PLACE
STAMP
HERE

Welcome
to School

<fold here>

To:

_____

_____

_____

_____

PLACE
STAMP
HERE

Welcome
to School

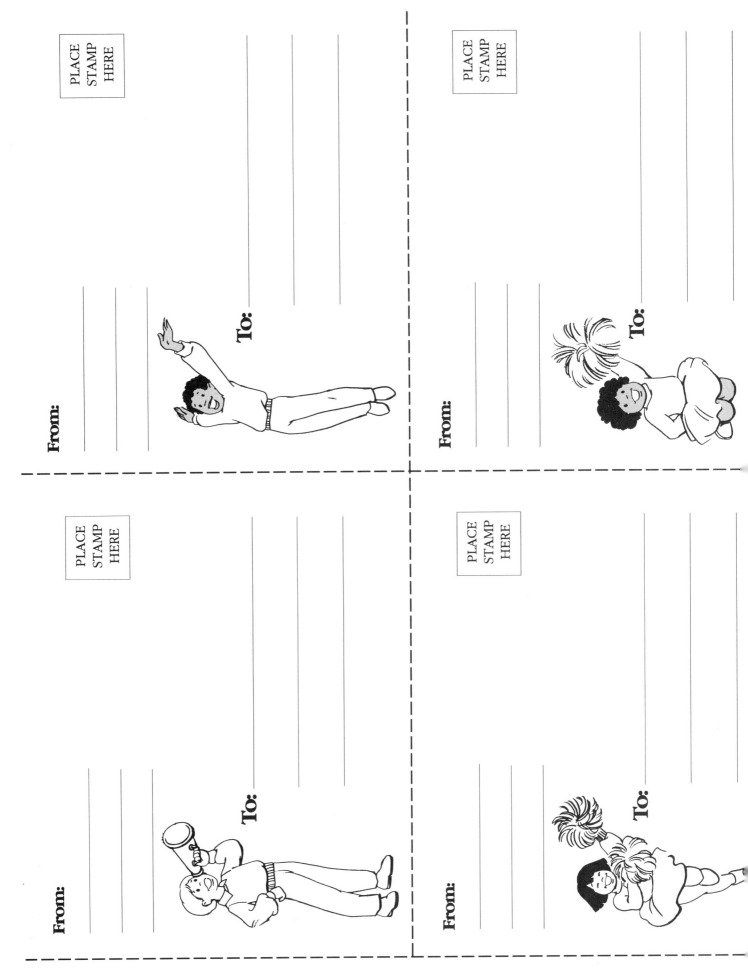

Dear _____,

Welcome to my class. I hope you have had a fun vacation. Here are some important facts about school.

First day of school _____

Time school (class) begins _____

Room Number _____

I'm looking forward to a great school year!

My name is _____

Dear _____,

Welcome to my class. I hope you have had a fun vacation. Here are some important facts about school.

First day of school _____

Time school (class) begins _____

Room Number _____

I'm looking forward to a great school year!

My name is _____

Dear _____,

Welcome to my class. I hope you have had a fun vacation. Here are some important facts about school.

First day of school _____

Time school (class) begins _____

Room Number _____

I'm looking forward to a great school year!

My name is _____

Dear _____,

Welcome to my class. I hope you have had a fun vacation. Here are some important facts about school.

First day of school _____

Time school (class) begins _____

Room Number _____

I'm looking forward to a great school year!

My name is _____

Welcoming Phone Calls To Parents and Students

Even before the school year begins, get in the habit of calling parents with good news! Parents have been conditioned to expect the worst when they get a phone call from the teacher. Change this pattern. The goal of this welcoming telephone call is to establish positive communication with parents and to show your professionalism, enthusiasm, and concern for your students.

Plan Your Call Before You Dial

Before you call, write down all the points you want to cover with the parent.
1. Introduce yourself.
2. Explain the purpose of the phone call.
3. Relay important information.
4. Make positive comments.
5. Ask for parent comments.
6. After the phone call, evaluate it.

Calling Parents of Potential Problem Students

A phone call is also a perfect way to open up communication with parents of potential problem students. These parents are probably used to hearing from school only when there is a problem. This is your chance to show them that you are aware of past problems, and that by working together, these past patterns can be changed. Above all, send the message that you are confident that this will be a successful year for their child.

Before You Dial

Plan to address each of these points:

1. Begin with a statement of concern.

> *"Mrs. Smith, this is Mr. Green. I'm going to be Jake's 6th grade teacher. I wanted to speak to you before the school year begins because I want to make sure that this year is a successful one for your child."*

2. Get parental input concerning the problems of last year. Ask parents for their input and point of view about the problem. Let the parent know that you genuinely care how he or she feels about what went on the previous year.

> *"I would like to know your view of what went on last year and why it was not as successful for Jake as it could have been."*

3. Get parental input for what will be needed to make this year more successful. Listen to the parent's suggestions. Their insights might give you a real advantage in dealing with the student right on the first day.

> *"I'd like to know what you feel we need to do to insure Jake has a good year this year."*

Welcoming Phone Call
Planning Sheet

Student _____

Telephone _____

Parents _____

_____

1. Introduce yourself _____

_____

2. Purpose of phone call _____

_____

_____

3. Important information regarding back to school _____

_____

_____

4. Positive comment about working together _____ _____

_____

_____

5. Parent comments _____

_____

_____

6. (Optional) Speak to student _____

_____

_____

7. Evaluation of phone call _____

_____

_____

Date _____

Welcoming Phone Call
(to parents of potential problem students)
Planning Sheet

Student _____

Parent(s) _____

Phone # _____

1. Introduce yourself _____

_____

2. Begin with a statement of concern _____

_____

3. Ask for parental input about previous problem _____

_____

4. Parent response _____

_____

5. Parent attitude: overwhelmed, angry, unable to deal with problem, other? _____

_____

6. Solicit parent suggestions and support _____

_____

7. Parent suggestions _____

_____

8. Thank parent for input and support _____

9. Give pertinent information about first day of school _____

_____

10. (Optional) Speak with child _____

_____

11. Evaluation of phone call _____

_____

Parents On Your Side - Resource Materials Workbook

Communicating Your Expectations to Parents

The First Week of School

The first week of school is a time for teachers and students to get acquainted. By teaching students how you expect them to behave in class, how you expect them to work in class, and how you expect them to do their homework, you will have laid the foundation for a successful school year.

If parents are to be actively involved, they too must be made aware of your behavioral and academic expectations. This foundation is equally as important as the one you build with students. Send home a copy of your discipline plan and your homework policy, along with a letter to introduce yourself. Because you will be an influential person in their children's lives for the next school year, it is important that they have an opportunity to learn about you.

Letter of Introduction

Use pages 20 and 21 to share information about yourself and your plans for the upcoming school year in a one-page letter of introduction. This upbeat, enthusiastic letter should include:
• information about your professional background,
• anything about your personal life that might be of interest (hobbies, travels, etc.),
• an overview of your educational plans for the upcoming school year and any special activities (field trips, science fair, etc.),
• a statement expressing your confidence in the success you expect for all your students this year.

Dear Parents,

My name is Mr. Robert Miller, and I will be your child's 6th grade teacher this year. You and I will be spending more time with your child in the upcoming school year than any other adult. Because of this, I'd like to take this opportunity to tell you a few things about myself—both personally and professionally.

I was born and raised in a small town in northern Minnesota, the "Land of 10,000 Lakes." I still love to fish streams in summer and go ice fishing in winter. I received my B.A. degree in Elementary Education from Minnesota State. I taught five years in Minneapolis before moving here seven years ago. This will be my eighth year teaching for the Maplewood School District.

This school year is going to be an exciting one. With the special assistance of my instructional aide, Mrs. Marquez, we will continue our successful schoolwide reading program. Besides the reading we do in class, our goal is for each student to read at least one free reading book a month (from the suggested reading list). Students will report on these books in a variety of exciting and entertaining ways (from puppet shows to illustrated reports).

Students will be learning many math concepts this year, including basic geometry. A "Math Olympics Day" will be held with sixth graders from all over the school district competing. The annual spring Science Fair promises to be a hit again this year. Our course of study in social studies will be world geography. Students will be asked to choose a country for their in-depth country report. An "International Banquet" with students preparing foods from many nations is planned as the culminating activity for the country report. Parents are invited, so get your appetites ready for next May's feast. Because so many things will be happening throughout the year, I will keep you updated through a "calendar of events" letter that will come home at the end of each month.

Parents are the most important people in a child's life, and we need to work together for the benefit of your child. I need you to support my academic, homework and discipline efforts here at school. In return, I will keep you informed about all aspects of your child's experiences at school. With school and home working together, I know that each and every student can have his or her most successful school year yet. I'm looking forward to meeting you personally at Back-to-School Night on September 30th.

Sincerely,

Mr. Robert Miller

Looking Forward to a Great Year!

Dear Parents,

My name is Mrs. Ann Ryan, and I will be your child's 10th grade English teacher this year. Because I will be spending an hour each day with your child, I'd like to take this opportunity to tell you a few things about myself both personally and professionally.

I was born and raised in a small town in southern Wisconsin. I received my B.A. and M.A. degrees in English from the University of Wisconsin. I taught five years in Milwaukee before moving here seven years ago. This will be my eighth year teaching for the Maplewood High School District and my third year teaching sophomore English.

I have always had a great love of literature and the arts. During my summer vacations I spend much time reading and attending plays and other theatrical performances. My nose is not always in a book, however. My favorite pastime now is rollerblading. Every weekend my husband and I skate through the park.

I have many exciting plans for my sophomore English class this year. Our readings and discussions will include plays by William Shakespeare and novels by William Saroyan, John Steinbeck and Pearl S. Buck. We will learn about Greek mythology and how it has influenced modern writers. Besides the reading we do in class, our goal is for each student to read at least one free reading book a month (from the suggested reading list). Students will report on these books in a variety of exciting and entertaining ways.

Parents are the most important people in a child's life, and we need to work together for the benefit of your child. I need you to support my academic, homework and discipline efforts here at school. In return, I will keep you informed about all aspects of your child's experiences at school. With school and home working together, I know that each and every student can have his or her most successful school year yet. I'm looking forward to meeting you personally at Back-to-School Night on September 30th.

Sincerely,

Mrs. Ann Ryan

Looking Forward to a Great New Year!

Looking Forward to a Great Year!

Why You Need a Classroom Discipline Plan

From the very first day, students must know how you expect them to behave in school and what they can expect from you. This plan is a fair and consistent way to deal with any behavior problems. It must be developed before school begins, taught to students the first day of school, and given to parents on the very same day.

Your discipline plan is an integral part of your parent involvement plan. It lets parents know exactly how their children are to behave, what will happen when they do behave, what will happen when they don't, and how parents will be involved.

What is a discipline plan?

A discipline plan consists of three parts:

1. The rules that students must follow at all times. There should be no more than five rules and they must be observable.

2. The consequences that will result when a student chooses not to follow the rules. These consequences are progressively more severe if a student continues to break rules. Latter consequences must include parent contact and a conference with the principal.

3. The rewards students will receive when they follow the rules. These rewards can range from verbal approval to the awarding of special privileges.

Sample Classroom Discipline Plan for an Elementary Classroom

Classroom Rules
1. Follow directions.
2. Keep hands, feet and objects to yourself.
3. No teasing or name calling.

Consequences
The first time a student breaks a rule ....Verbal warning
The second time a student breaks a rule ...Last in line to recess
The third time a student breaks a rule ....Time-out area (5 minutes)
The fourth time a student breaks a rule ....Teacher calls parent
The fifth time a student breaks a rule ....Send to principal

Severe Behavior Clause
When a student severely misbehaves (such as hitting another student, threatening teacher, etc.).......................Immediately send to principal

Rewards
Students who follow the rules will receive:
     Praise
     Positive notes sent home
     Small rewards
     Star or sticker on a chart
     Class parties
     Wear "Good Behavior Badge" for a day
     Photograph in the office's "Behavior Hall of Fame"

Which rules, consequences and rewards are appropriate?

The elements of your classroom discipline plan must be comfortable for you and must be age appropriate. Don't choose a rule or a consequence that you won't enforce 100% of the time. Consistency is the key to the success of any discipline plan. Choose rules, consequences and rewards that you will implement throughout the school year.

Sample Classroom Discipline Plan for a Secondary Classroom

Rules
1. Follow directions the first time they are given.
2. Bring books, notebooks, pen and pencils to class.
3. No teasing or name calling.

Consequences

The first time a student breaks a rule	Verbal warning
The second time a student breaks a rule	Last student dismissed + 30 seconds
The third time a student breaks a rule	Last student dismissed + 60 seconds
The fourth time a student breaks a rule	Teacher calls parent
The fifth time a student breaks a rule	Send to principal

Severe Behavior Clause
When a student severely misbehaves (such as hitting another student, threatening teacher, etc.)......................Immediately send to principal

Rewards
Students who follow the classroom rules will receive:
> Praise
> Positive notes sent home
> Privilege coupons
> Class privilege (free time on Friday)

How do I communicate my classroom discipline plan to students?

On the first day of school, designate a time to teach students the rules. They must be made aware of what will happen if they choose to break rules and how you will provide positive reinforcement when they follow the rules. Each student should have a copy of the rules to keep at his or her desk. A copy of the plan (rules, consequences and rewards) should be posted at the front of the room on a sheet of poster board. Make sure this chart is visible from anywhere in the classroom. Another copy of your plan should be stapled to the inside front cover or your lesson plan book for substitutes.

How do I communicate my classroom discipline plan to parents?

Send a discipline plan letter home to parents the first day of school. Include a "sign-off and return to school" portion at the bottom of the letter. This indicates that the parent has read and discussed the plan with the student. Use the letterhead on page 25 for your letter.

MY CLASSROOM DISCIPLINE PLAN

Important
PLEASE READ!

Dear Parent,

I am delighted that your child_____ is in my class this year. With your encouragement, your child will be a part of many exciting and rewarding experiences this academic year.

Since lifelong success depends in part on self-discipline, I have developed a Classroom Discipline Plan which affords every student guidance in making good decisions about their behavior and thus an opportunity to learn in a positive, nurturing class environment. Your child deserves the most positive educational climate possible for his/her growth, and I know that, together we will make a difference in this process. The plan below outlines our classroom rules, possible rewards and consequences for appropriate and inappropriate behavior. They are:

Rules:

1. Follow directions the first time given.
2. Keeps hands, feet and objects to yourself.
3. No cussing or teasing.

To encourage students to follow our class rules, I will support appropriate behavior with praise, happy notes home and positive phone calls home.

However, if a student chooses to break a rule, the following steps will be taken:

1st consequence	Warning
2nd consequence	1 minute after class or lost recess time
3rd consequence	2 minutes after class or lost recess time
4th consequence	Call parents
5th consequence	Send to principal

Please be assured that my goal is to work with parents the way I would want my children's teachers to work with me. Also, I am available to conference if you need to meet with me before or after school.

Please ask your child to review this classroom plan with you, and then sign and return the form below. Thank you for joining our winning home/school team.

_____
Teacher's Signature   Room Number   Date

I have read_____Classroom Discipline Plan and discussed it with him/her.

_____
Parent/Guardian Signature   Date

Comments _____

_____

_____

Why You Need a Homework Policy

One night, several nights, or every night of the school week students bring home assignments to complete and return to school. With parents on your side, homework will become a positive extension of school. How do you get parent support? It's easy. Explain your reasons for giving homework, the types of assignments that will be given, how students are expected to complete assignments and what role the parents can play in the homework process. This home/school connection can become a source of positive interaction between teacher and parents – if you bring parents into the homework process at the beginning of the school year.

How to communicate your homework expectations to students

Before you assign the first homework assignment of the year, your students must be taught beginning homework and study skills. Students must know how assignments are to be completed, when assignments will be given, when they are due and what happens if work is not turned in on time.

Your first homework assignment of the year should be for each of your students to take home the classroom discipline and homework policy letters, discuss them with their parent(s), get their parent(s) signatures on the sign-off portions of the letters, cut them off and return them to class the following day.

How do I communicate my homework expectations to parents

On the first day of school send home a copy of your homework policy with each student. Use the homework policy letterhead on page 30. Your homework policy should clearly state your expectations for everyone involved in the homework process: student, teacher and parents.

Your homework policy should include the following information:

1. Explanation of why homework is assigned. Some homework prepares students for upcoming topics, while other assignments reinforce skills and material already learned in class. Homework teaches students to work independently and assume responsibility for their own work.

2. Explanation of the types of homework you will assign. It's important to let everyone know the homework you assign requires only those skills students have already learned. Explain daily homework assignments (answering chapter questions), weekly homework assignments (spelling stories due every Friday) and long-range assignments (reports and projects).

3. Information for parents on the amount and frequency of homework. Your homework policy should include the days of the week on which you will assign homework and the amount of time it should take students to complete homework.

4. Guidelines for when and how students are to complete homework. Both students and parents must be aware of these expectations. Some typical expectations include:
• All assignments will be finished completely.
• Students will do homework on their own and to the best of their ability.
• Students will turn in work that is neatly done.
• Students will turn in homework on time.
• Students are responsible for making up homework assignments missed due to absence.

5. Statement that you will keep a record of assignments completed and not completed. Recordkeeping is imperative to the success of your homework program. Knowing that you keep accurate records keeps everyone accountable.

6. Explanation of how homework will affect student's grades. Will it be averaged as a percentage of each subject's grade or will it be part of the citizenship grade? Whatever grading system you use, it must be stated in your homework policy.

7. Information for parents and students about test schedules. Do you give regularly scheduled tests every week? In elementary school, Friday is often designated as "spelling test day." In secondary schools, "pop quizzes" on the week's work are often given weekly. Let parents know about these regularly scheduled tests. Also explain to parents that you will send home adequate written notice before important subject area tests are given.

8. Specific information on how you will positively reinforce students who complete homework. Good homework skills should be rewarded with a variety of positives: verbal praise, awards, notes home to parents and special class activities.

9. Explanation of what you will do when students do not complete homework. Spell out the actions you will take when students do not complete homework. Here are some examples of action taken when a student does not complete homework:
• Parent(s) must sign completed homework every night.
• Student will miss recess to complete homework. (elementary)
• Student will be given study-hall detention to complete homework assignments. (secondary)
• Student will complete homework after school.
• Student's grade will be lowered.

10. Clarification of what is expected of the parent. Parent support is essential for the success of your homework program. Give them at-home guidelines for dealing with homework. Parents should:
• Establish homework as a top priority for their child.
• Make sure that their child does homework in a quiet environment.
• Establish a time every day during which homework must be done.
• Give their child positive support when homework is completed.
• Not allow their child to get out of doing homework.
• Contact you if their child has problems with homework.

MY CLASSROOM HOMEWORK POLICY

To the family of _____,

I have written this letter to answer any questions you may have regarding homework assigned in my classroom. Please read this letter, discuss it with your child, and return the bottom portion to school with your signature.

Why do I assign homework? I believe homework is important because it is a valuable tool in helping students make the most of their experience in school. Homework helps reinforce what has been learned in class, prepares students for upcoming lessons, teaches responsibility and helps students develop positive study habits.

When will homework be assigned? Homework will be assigned Tuesday and Thursday nights. Assignments should take no more than one-half hour to complete each night, not including studying for spelling tests which are given each Friday. Students should read at least 15 minutes every night in a library book of their choice.

What are your child's homework responsibilities? I expect students to do their best job on each homework assignment. I expect homework to be neat, not sloppy. All written work should be done in pencil. I expect homework to be completely finished by classtime the following morning.

What are my responsibilities? I will check all homework assignments and record them in my grade book. I will support good homework habits by giving praise and other incentives.

What are a parent's homework responsibilities? Parents are the key to making homework a positive experience for their children. Therefore, I ask that you make homework a top priority at home, provide necessary supplies and a quiet homework environment, set aside a time everyday when homework should be done, provide praise and support, not allow your child to avoid doing homework, and contact me if you notice a problem.

What will happen if students do not complete their homework assignments? If students choose not to do their homework, I will ask that parents begin checking and signing completed homework each night. If students still choose not to complete their homework, they also choose to lose certain privileges. After three homework assignments have not been turned in, or turned in incomplete, the parent will be contacted.

What about legitimate reasons for a student not completing a homework assignment? If there is a legitimate reason why a student is unable to finish the assignment, please send a note to me on the date the homework is due stating the reason it was not completed. The note must be signed by the parent.

Thanks for your support, *Miss Jones*

— —

I have read and discussed this homework policy with my child.

Signed _____

Date _____

MY CLASSROOM HOMEWORK POLICY

PLEASE READ!

Dear Parents,

I have written this letter to answer any questions you may have regarding homework assigned in my classroom. Please read this letter, discuss it with your child and return the bottom portion to school with your signature.

Why do I assign homework? I believe homework is important because it is a valuable tool in helping students make the most of their experience in school. Homework helps reinforce what has been learned in class, prepares students for upcoming lessons, teaches responsibility and helps students develop positive study habits.

When will homework be assigned? Homework will be assigned Monday, Wednesday and Thursday nights. Assignments should take no more than forty-five minutes to complete each night, not including studying for mid-terms and finals. Students should read at least 15 minutes every night in a library book of their choice. Written and oral book reports will be due in November, February and May.

What are your child's homework responsibilities? I expect students to do their best job on each homework assignment. I expect homework to be neat, not sloppy. All daily written work should be done in pencil. All reports should be completed in ink or typewritten. I expect all homework to be completely finished by classtime the following day.

What are my responsibilities? I will check all homework assignments and record them in my grade book. I will support good homework habits by giving praise and other incentives.

What are a parent's homework responsibilities? Parents are the key to making homework a positive experience for their children. Therefore, I ask that you make homework a top priority at home, provide necessary supplies and a quiet homework environment, set aside a time everyday when homework should be done, provide praise and support, help your child get to the library when necessary, not allow your child to avoid doing homework, and contact me if you notice a problem.

What will happen if students do not complete their homework assignments? If students choose not to do their homework, I will ask that parents begin checking and signing completed homework each night. If students still choose not to complete their homework, they also choose to lose certain privileges. After three homework assignments have not been turned in, or turned in incomplete, the parent will be contacted.

What about legitimate reasons for a student not completing a homework assignment? If there is a legitimate reason why a student is unable to finish the assignment, please send a note to me on the date the homework is due stating the reason it was not completed. The note must be signed by the parent.

Thanks for your support,   Mr. Cowan

- -

I have read and discussed this homework policy with my child.

Signed _____

Date _____

More Handy Handouts for the First Week of School

Use page 31 or 32 to relay information about the school year. Include school name, address and telephone number; principal's name; your name and room number; daily schedule; holidays; conference periods and report card schedules; school programs and class activities.

- -

School _____   Address _____

Telephone Number _____   Principal _____

Teacher _____   Room Number _____

School Starts _____   Lunch _____   Dismissal _____

School Year CALENDAR

September _____   March _____

_____   _____

_____   _____

October _____   April _____

_____   _____

_____   _____

November _____   May _____

_____   _____

_____   _____

December _____   June _____

_____   _____

_____   _____

January _____   July _____

_____   _____

_____   _____

February _____   August _____

_____   _____

_____   _____

CALENDAR

Making Your "Back-to-School" Night a Parent Involvement Success

What better way to get parents on your side than at Back-to-School Night? By setting the right mood, getting everyone involved, and preparing an informative, easy-to-follow talk about the school year, you can create the perfect opportunity to make allies of every parent in the classroom. It requires planning, but the outcome is definitely worth the effort. Follow the simple steps in this section to a successful Back-to-School Night.

Back-to-School Night: Step 1

Make a commitment to do all you can to encourage full parent participation.

Invitations and Reminders

Pull out all the stops! Blitz your parents with personalized invitations that contain a tantalizing preview of what the night will bring. Get your students excited about the event, too. Their enthusiasm could be just the trick to get apathetic parents into the classroom. If possible, coordinate a schoolwide babysitting service for Back-to-School Night. You'll see better attendance. Don't forget to inform parents about this special service on the invitation. Send reminder slips home a day or two before Back-to-School Night. These days, many parents will need a gentle reminder. (See the Back-to-School Night invitations on pages 35 and 36, and the reproducible reminder slips on page 37.)

Boost parent attendance with parent motivators.

The first objective of Back-to-School Night is to get parents there. Try these activities to motivate parent participation:

• Back-to-School Night Raffle

Attending parents place signed raffle tickets in a jar. During the next school day, the teacher pulls several tickets from the jar. Winning ticket holders are awarded school supplies (markers, picture dictionary, compass). Announce the raffle before Back-to-School Night so students can help motivate their parents to participate. (See raffle tickets on page 38.)

• Back-to-School Night Lotto

Parents who attend Back-to-School Night sign their names in spaces on the special lotto board (see page 39). The teacher pulls winning numbers the next day and awards prizes to students whose parents' names were drawn.

• Back-to-School Night Bonus Tickets

Any student whose parent(s) attends Back-to-School Night receives a ticket entitling him or her to a special privilege or award, such as free reading time, a pencil or a notepad. Use the Back-to-School Night sign-in sheet on page 40 to determine who gets a ticket.

For parents who can't attend Back-to-School Night...

Some parents will be unable to attend (because of work, illness, prior commitments, etc.). Don't give up on them. Send home a note in which you invite them to join in the raffle (or whatever incentive you use). This avoids penalizing any student in the class. It also lets parents know that you will go that extra mile to keep them informed about their child's education. Use the notes on page 42 to reach out to those parents who couldn't attend.

You're invited to

Back-to-School Night

Date _____

Time _____

Place _____

This will be a very special night, so let's "team up" for the children.
Looking forward to seeing you.

Check a box, sign, tear off and return to school with your child.

☐ **Yes, I plan to be there.**

☐ **Sorry, I am unable to attend.**

Name _____ Parent of _____

You're invited to

Back-to-School Night

Date _____

Time _____

Place _____

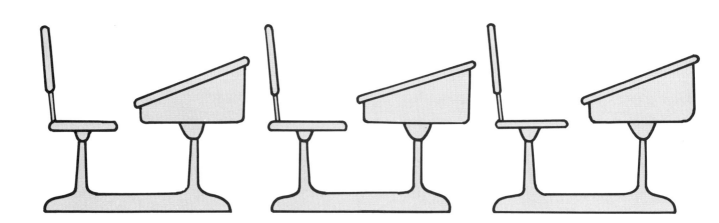

Follow this schedule so that you can meet your child's teachers and learn about the upcoming school year.

Period	Class	Teacher	Room #	Time

**This will be a very special night,
so let's team up for our students.**

Looking forward to seeing you.

Parents On Your Side - Resource Materials Workbook

Please remember...

Back-to-School Night

Date _____

Time _____

Place _____

Make this a winning school year by attending.
Our goal is **100% parent participation**!

- -

Please remember...

Back-to-School Night

Date _____

Time _____

Place _____

Make this a winning school year by attending.
Our goal is **100% parent participation**!

- -

Please remember...

Back-to-School Night

Date _____

Time _____

Place _____

Make this a winning school year by attending.
Our goal is **100% parent participation**!

- -

Please remember...

Back-to-School Night

Date _____

Time _____

Place _____

Make this a winning school year by attending.
Our goal is **100% parent participation**!

Rah! Rah! Rah!

Give a cheer!
It's very nice to
have you here!

Enter my child, _____,
in the **Back-to-School Night Raffle!**

Rah! Rah! Rah!

Give a cheer!
It's very nice to
have you here!

Enter my child, _____,
in the **Back-to-School Night Raffle!**

Rah! Rah! Rah!

Give a cheer!
It's very nice to
have you here!

Enter my child, _____,
in the **Back-to-School Night Raffle!**

Rah! Rah! Rah!

Give a cheer!
It's very nice to
have you here!

Enter my child, _____,
in the **Back-to-School Night Raffle!**

Rah! Rah! Rah!

Give a cheer!
It's very nice to
have you here!

Enter my child, _____,
in the **Back-to-School Night Raffle!**

Rah! Rah! Rah!

Give a cheer!
It's very nice to
have you here!

Enter my child, _____,
in the **Back-to-School Night Raffle!**

Rah! Rah! Rah!

Give a cheer!
It's very nice to
have you here!

Enter my child, _____,
in the **Back-to-School Night Raffle!**

Rah! Rah! Rah!

Give a cheer!
It's very nice to
have you here!

Enter my child, _____,
in the **Back-to-School Night Raffle!**

Let's play...
Back-to-School Night
LOTTO

	A	B	C	D	E
1					
2					
3					
4					
5					
6					
7					
8					

**Parents, please sign your child's name
in one blank square on the Lotto Board above.**

Welcome to
Back-to-School Night

Please sign in.

1. _____		23. _____
2. _____		24. _____
3. _____		25. _____
4. _____		26. _____
5. _____		27. _____
6. _____		28. _____
7. _____		29. _____
8. _____		30. _____
9. _____		31. _____
10. _____		32. _____
11. _____		33. _____
12. _____		34. _____
13. _____		35. _____
14. _____		36. _____
15. _____		37. _____
16. _____		38. _____
17. _____		39. _____
18. _____		40. _____
19. _____		41. _____
20. _____		42. _____
21. _____		43. _____
22. _____		44. _____

Back-to-School Night
BONUS TICKET
This ticket entitles you to

_____

Back-to-School Night
BONUS TICKET
This ticket entitles you to

_____

Back-to-School Night
BONUS TICKET
This ticket entitles you to

_____

Back-to-School Night
BONUS TICKET
This ticket entitles you to

_____

Back-to-School Night
BONUS TICKET
This ticket entitles you to

_____

Back-to-School Night
BONUS TICKET
This ticket entitles you to

_____

Back-to-School Night
BONUS TICKET
This ticket entitles you to

_____

Back-to-School Night
BONUS TICKET
This ticket entitles you to

_____

Back-to-School Night News

To the family of _____ ,

We missed you at Back-to-School Night. Here's a summary of what you missed:

_____

_____

_____

_____

_____

_____

_____

_____

_____

Sincerely, _____

Please fill out the coupon at the bottom of this note and send it back to school as soon as possible.

- -

I received your note about Back-to-School Night.

Comments: _____

_____

_____

Thank you,

From the family of _____   _____
                        Student's name   Parent signature

Create an inviting classroom environment that says, "Welcome to our room."

Make a positive first impression with parents by creating an inviting, friendly atmosphere that helps parents feel involved and welcome. Get your students involved in making posters, banners and name tags. If you roll out the welcome mat on Back-to-School Night, you can create an atmosphere that says, "You're welcome here anytime." Don't forget to display your daily class schedule (on the chalkboard or a poster). Displays of work completed and curriculum are important visual aids when discussing your upcoming academic program. In elementary school, make a point of putting name tags on each child's desk. Encourage parents to sit at their own child's desk or table, and you will be able to make the connection of parent with child more readily.

Parents On Your Side - Resource Materials Workbook

We've got a winning team...

Super Students!
Involved Parents! • Terrific Teachers!

Go team, go!

Name(s) of parent(s):

<fold here>

This desk belongs to:

Name(s) of parent(s):

<fold here>

This desk belongs to:

Parent Name Tags

Back-to-School Night: Step 3
Plan exactly what you will say.

You will have a captive audience at Back-to-School Night. Inform them. Entertain them. Show them that this is just the beginning of a dynamic year in which you and they can team up to become partners in their children's education. To insure you cover everything in your presentation, prepare an outline of exactly what you will say. This will calm your nerves and keep you on track.

Be sure to include:
• an overview of your daily routine.
• an overview of your academic plans for the school year in all major subjects.
• an explanation of your discipline plan.
• an explanation of your homework policy.
  • information about arrival and dismissal times, lunch, absences, special services, etc.

A major goal of Back-to-School Night is to get parents interested and involved in their child's education. Your presentation should convince parents that through their influence they can help children achieve their highest potential. Use the sample outline forms on pages 49 to 52 to help organize your presentation.

Back-to-School Night
Presentation Outline (K-6)

1. Greeting and welcome _____

_____

_____

2. Emphasize to parents that they are the most important people in their child's life.

_____

_____

_____

3. Explain when and how you will communicate with parents.

_____

_____

_____

4. Explain your daily routine and academic program.

_____

_____

Subject:_____

Subject:_____

Subject:_____

Subject:_____

Subject:_____

5. Describe your Classroom Discipline Plan.

_____

_____

_____

6. Describe your Homework Policy.

_____

_____

_____

_____

7. Tell parents exactly how you need them to support your academic, discipline and homework efforts.

_____

_____

_____

8. Give parents suggestions for how they can help at home.

_____

_____

_____

9. Invite parents to help at school.

_____

_____

10. Optional activities:
• Take parents on a tour of the classroom.
• Show parents a video or slides of students in their daily classroom routines.
• Play a tape recording of students discussing classroom activities.
• Have parents write a note to their child and leave it on the desk.

• Other _____

_____

11. Hand out Parent Handbooks, noting specific information not covered in your presentation.

12. Ask for questions. _____

Notes: _____

_____

_____

_____

_____

13. Remind parents about raffle or lotto games.

_____

_____

14. End on a positive, caring note stressing the importance of parents and teachers working as a team.

_____

_____

_____

_____

_____

Back-to-School Night Presentation Outline (7-12)

1. Greeting and welcome _____

_____

2. Emphasize to parents that they are the most important people in their child's life.

_____

_____

_____

3. Explain when and how you will communicate with parents.

_____

_____

_____

4. Explain what your academic program will include for the upcoming semester (school year) .

_____

_____

_____

_____

_____

5. Describe your Classroom Discipline Plan.

_____

_____

_____

_____

_____

6. Describe your Homework Policy.

_____

_____

_____

_____

_____

7. Tell parents exactly how you need them to support your academic, discipline and homework efforts.

_____

_____

_____

_____

_____

8. Give parents suggestions for how they can help at home.

_____

_____

_____

_____

9. Hand out parent fact sheets that cover specific information covered and not covered in your presentation.

10. Ask for questions. _____

Notes: _____

_____

_____

_____

_____

_____

_____

_____

_____

11. End on a positive, caring note stressing the importance of parents and teachers working as a team.

_____

_____

_____

_____

_____

Back-to-School Night: Step 4

Create and distribute a Parent Handbook.

Hand out a packet of information that parents can take home with them. The information in the parent packet might include a summary of the information from your presentation and (depending on your grade level) some of the following information:

- Class list
- Staff list
- Map of the school
- Schoolwide rules
- Daily classroom schedule
- Grade level curriculum
- Discipline plan
- Homework policy
- Suggested reading lists
- Manuscript/cursive writing guide
- Policies: absences, medical appointments, making up classwork
- Blank teacher/parent communication forms
- Tips on how to help a child study at home
- Blank notes for parents when reporting their child's absence
- Volunteer request forms

Pages 54 to 62 contain reproducibles and letterheads for many of the items you might include in your Parent Handbook—from the handbook cover to a specialized volunteer request form.

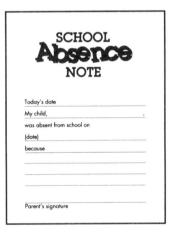

Back-to-School Handbook for Parents

_____

Teacher

_____

Grade

_____

Room Number

_____

School Year

_____

School

_____

School Phone

_____

Parent-to-Teacher Communication Form

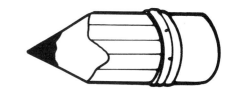

To: _____

Comments: _____

_____

_____

_____

_____

_____

_____

_____

_____

_____

_____

From: _____ Date: _____

- -

Teacher-to-Parent Reply

To: _____

Comments: _____

_____

_____

_____

_____

_____

_____

_____

_____

_____

From: _____ Date: _____

Power Reading Tip Sheet

To do well in all subjects at school, children must have strong reading comprehension skills. This means that they must be able to understand what they are reading. You can help your child develop these skills with a technique called Power Reading. Here's how it works.

First, read to your child.
Read aloud to your child for five minutes. Be sure that the book from which you are reading is at your child's reading level. Pronounce words carefully and clearly, and make appropriate pauses for periods and commas.

Next, listen to your child read.
Have your child continue reading the same book aloud for another five minutes. He or she should begin at the point where you stopped reading. Remind your child to take it slowly and read so that the words make sense. This is why your oral reading is so important. It's setting an example for your child. Don't stop and correct your child while he or she is reading.

Finally, ask questions about what was read.
Check how well your child was listening and reading by asking general questions about the material you read aloud and the material he or she read aloud. Talk about the story together.

Hold a Power Reading session with your child as often as possible. It's an excellent way to improve reading skills and demonstrate the importance you place on reading. Start with a book that's of particular interest to your child and continue using this same book for Power Reading sessions until it is completed.

Chart your Power Reading sessions for one month.
Mark this chart each time you and your child have a Power Reading session in one month.

Month of:

Sun.	Mon.	Tues.	Wed.	Thur.	Fri.	Sat.

Map of Our School

Helping Your Child at Home

SCHOOL POLICIES

Absences

_____

_____

_____

_____

Medical Appointments

_____

_____

_____

Administering of Medicine

_____

_____

_____

_____

Tardiness

_____

_____

_____

_____

_____

SCHOOL Absence NOTE

Today's date _____

My child, _____ ,

was absent from school on

(date) _____

because _____

_____

_____

_____

Parent's signature _____

SCHOOL Absence NOTE

Today's date _____

My child, _____ ,

was absent from school on

(date) _____

because _____

_____

_____

_____

Parent's signature _____

SCHOOL Absence NOTE

Today's date _____

My child, _____ ,

was absent from school on

(date) _____

because _____

_____

_____

_____

Parent's signature _____

SCHOOL Absence NOTE

Today's date _____

My child, _____ ,

was absent from school on

(date) _____

because _____

_____

_____

_____

Parent's signature _____

Calling all Volunteers

WE COULD USE A HELPING HAND

Here's how:

_____

_____

_____

_____

_____

_____

_____

_____

Thanks,

- -

☐ I'd love to help.
☐ I can help at home.
☐ I'm unable to volunteer at this time.

Parent's signature _____

Back-to-School Night Extras

Parent-to-Child Telegrams

Have each parent write a brief note to their child saying what they liked most about Back-to-School Night. These notes should be collected and handed back to your students the following day. You might get some great insights into your presentation and program from these parent comment sheets. Use the reproducible on page 64.

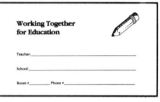

Teacher Calling Cards

Back-to-School Night is the perfect opportunity to give each attending parent a personalized business card. Reproduce these Teaching Calling Cards on quality paper stock after you have typed or neatly printed your name, room number, school name and school telephone number on each card on the master copy on page 65. Some teachers choose to put their home phone numbers on the cards, too. Use your judgement. Encourage parents to keep the cards in their wallets. In case a parent needs to contact you concerning their child, your phone number will be right at hand.

Back-to-School Night Follow Up

Let parents know how much you appreciated their participation in Back-to-School Night. Several days after the event, send home a brief note (see page 66) thanking parents for coming and updating them on any item that might have come under discussion at Back-to-School Night. A reply section for parent comments allows those parents who find it difficult to speak up in group to get their message across.

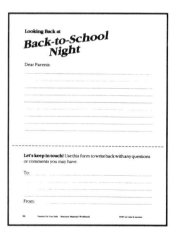

Just Between Us!

Here's an important message for _____
about Back-to-School Night.

_____

_____

_____

_____

_____

Signed _____

- -

Just Between Us!

Here's an important message for _____
about Back-to-School Night.

_____

_____

_____

_____

_____

Signed

**Working Together
for Education**

Teacher:_____

School:_____

Room #_____ Phone #_____

**Working Together
for Education**

Teacher:_____

School:_____

Room #_____ Phone #_____

**Let's work together!
We Can Make the Difference**

Teacher:_____

School:_____

Room #_____ Phone #_____

**Let's work together!
We Can Make the Difference**

Teacher:_____

School:_____

Room #_____ Phone #_____

**Success in education
is a team effort,
so let's work together!**

Teacher:_____

School:_____

Room #_____ Phone #_____

**Success in education
is a team effort,
so let's work together!**

Teacher:_____

School:_____

Room #_____ Phone #_____

**Working Together
for Education**

Teacher:_____

School:_____

Room #_____ Phone #_____

**Working Together
for Education**

Teacher:_____

School:_____

Room #_____ Phone #_____

**Let's work together!
We Can Make the Difference**

Teacher:_____

School:_____

Room #_____ Phone #_____

**Let's work together!
We Can Make the Difference**

Teacher:_____

School:_____

Room #_____ Phone #_____

Teacher Calling Cards

Looking Back at
Back-to-School Night

Dear Parents:

_____

_____

_____

_____

_____

_____

_____

_____

- -

Let's keep in touch! Use this form to write back with any questions or comments you may have.

To: _____

_____

_____

From: _____

Positive Parent Communication
Ideas for the Entire School

By communicating positive news to parents throughout the school year, the message is sent that you truly are concerned about their children. Your initial efforts at positive parent communication (phone calls, notes, letters about your academic and behavioral expectations for the upcoming year, and Back-to-School Night) are the perfect way to start the year. Commit yourself to consistently and positively communicating with all your parents throughout the school year.

When should I communicate with parents?

In order to reach all parents, you need to organize your efforts. Positive communication won't happen if you don't schedule it.

Which positive communications work best?

Effective teachers use a variety of techniques to positively communicate with parents. These have proven to be very successful:
- Positive phone calls
- Notes, cards and letters
- Home visits
- Parent communication activities

Positive Phone Calls

A quick phone call updating parents on their child's success in school (academic, behavior or social) is a good habit to establish at the beginning of the year. If you make two phone calls a day (each call only five minutes in length), you can reach ten parents a week. At that rate (in a typical elementary classroom) you could contact each parent once a month. Secondary teachers would be able to contact each parent at least once a semester. If you get into the habit of phoning parents with good news, it won't be so difficult to call them when there is a problem to be solved.

Here are the points you'll want to cover in a positive phone call:

• **Describe the student's positive behavior.** Be specific. For example,

"Robin is off to a great start this year. She has completed all of her classwork and homework this week."

• **Describe how you feel about the student's positive behavior.** Let the parent know how pleased you are with the student's good behavior or academic performance. For example,

"I've very pleased that Brian is showing such improvement in his reading (algebra, chemistry) this year. His hard work is getting results."

• **Ask the parent to share the content of the phone call with their child.** For example,

"Please tell Robin that I called and how pleased I am with her work."

The Positive Phone Call Form on page 68 will help you schedule and prepare for these most effective parent contacts.

Positive Phone Call Form

1. Student _____ Phone # _____ Parent _____
    Positive behavior _____
    Your comments _____
    Parent's comments _____

2. Student _____ Phone # _____ Parent _____
    Positive behavior _____
    Your comments _____
    Parent's comments _____

3. Student _____ Phone # _____ Parent _____
    Positive behavior _____
    Your comments _____
    Parent's comments _____

4. Student _____ Phone # _____ Parent _____
    Positive behavior _____
    Your comments _____
    Parent's comments _____

5. Student _____ Phone # _____ Parent _____
    Positive behavior _____
    Your comments _____
    Parent's comments _____

6. Student _____ Phone # _____ Parent _____
    Positive behavior _____
    Your comments _____
    Parent's comments _____

7. Student _____ Phone # _____ Parent _____
    Positive behavior _____
    Your comments _____
    Parent's comments _____

8. Student _____ Phone # _____ Parent _____
    Positive behavior _____
    Your comments _____
    Parent's comments _____

9. Student _____ Phone # _____ Parent _____
    Positive behavior _____
    Your comments _____
    Parent's comments _____

10. Student _____ Phone # _____ Parent _____
    Positive behavior _____
    Your comments _____
    Parent's comments _____

Positive Notes, Cards and Letters

Be the "bearer of glad tidings" throughout the school year by giving parents positive feedback on their child's performance through notes, cards and letters. A brief note explaining something good about their child will go a long way in building good parent relations.

Get into the habit of sending home several notes each day. When a parent reaches into his or her child's backpack and retrieves a personal, positive note from school, the day takes on a warm glow. Keep those happy embers glowing in the homes of all your children and soon even the coolest of parents will warm up to you.

Here are a few hints:

• Keep a file of ready-to-use positive notes and preaddressed envelopes in your desk. Fill out an envelope for each student the first day of each month. By the end of the month, each envelope should have reached home with a positive message inside.

• Use the form on page 95 to keep track of your positive messages home. Staple it to the inside cover of your lesson plan book for easy access.

• When writing notes, address the parents by name and mention the child's name, too.

• Use a seasonal sticker to secure fold-a-notes (see page 70) or envelopes.

EXCITING NEWS
FROM SCHOOL!

FOR

PARENT'S NAME

SPECIAL NEWS
ABOUT A
VERY
SPECIAL STUDENT

— for —

PARENT'S NAME

Dear _____ **,**

PARENT'S NAME

_____

STUDENT'S NAME

had a _____ **day because**

_____

_____

_____

Signed _____ Date _____

Dear _____ **,**

PARENT'S NAME

_____

STUDENT'S NAME

had a Grade "A" day because

_____

_____

_____

Signed _____ Date _____

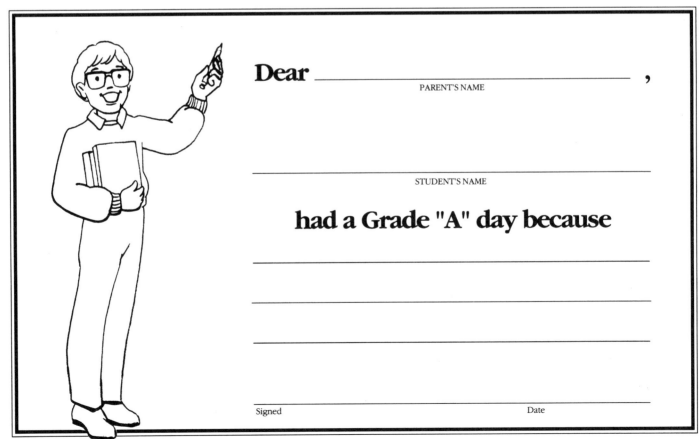

Attention: _____
PARENT'S NAME

I'm very proud to announce that

_____
STUDENT'S NAME

has made a BIG IMPROVEMENT in our classroom because

_____

_____

_____

_____

Signed   Date

To: _____
PARENT'S NAME

CONGRATULATIONS!

I'm pleased to announce that

_____
STUDENT'S NAME

had a GREAT DAY because

_____

_____

_____

Signed   Date

Congratulations, _____ **!**

Your child really

ACED

this assignment.

_____

_____

_____
Signed   Date

FYI

For Your Information

Dear _____ **,**

Your child, _____ **,**
has done an OUTSTANDING job
in my classroom.
I'm so pleased because

_____

_____

_____

_____
Signed   Date

SUPER STAR AWARD

presented to

_____

because

_____

_____

_____
Signed   Date

TNT

Tremendously Noteworthy Test

Dear _____,

Your child did a "dynamite" job on this test!

_____
Signed   Date

Birthday Greetings for Students and Parents

Student Birthday Cards

Recognize the birthdays of your students and their parents with birthday cards–from you! What better way to show you care than by sending home a birthday card?

Keep a class birthday list in your plan book so you can be prepared. The birthday cards on pages 77-78 will be a source of fun for the entire family.

To the teacher: Reproduce puzzle card on index card stock or construction paper. Write the student's name on the cake and sign your name at the bottom. Then

      cut

         it

           up

              into

                  puzzle

               pieces

and place them in an envelope. Student must put together the puzzle in order to read the birthday message.

Parent Birthday Cards

Have your students create a birthday card for each parent at the beginning of the year. Then file them away and send home when appropriate. The personalized cards on pages 79-80 will make a big splash when they're delivered. Reproduce the cards on sturdy paper, let the children color and decorate them with markers, glitter, or flowers, and then have them write a personal message to their parent.

Happy Birthday!

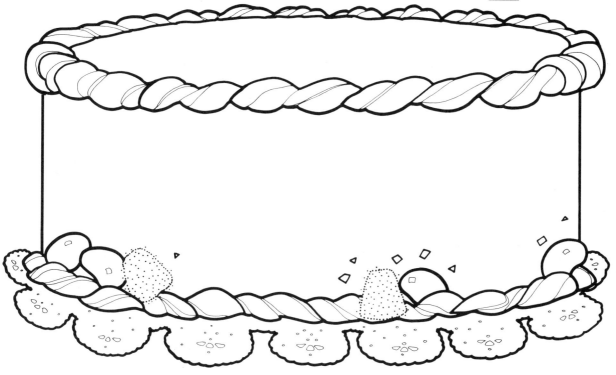

Many Happy Returns from Your Teacher,

– – – – – – –<fold here>– – – – – – – – – –

3 Cheers for _____

on Your Birthday!

— <fold here> —

HAPPY BIRTHDAY, MOM!

- - - - - - - <fold here> - - - - - - - - - -

HAPPY BIRTHDAY, DAD !

Parents On Your Side - Resource Materials Workbook

Get Well Messages

A card or quick phone call to check on a student's health and update parents on the child's classwork is a perfect opportunity for positive communication. Here's an example of a get well phone call:

Hello, Mrs. Wilson? This is Mary Johnson, David's teacher. We've missed David this week and I just wanted to give you a call and see how he's doing. Everyone in the class sends their best wishes. We're looking forward to having him back.

I know he may be concerned about the work he's missing, but tell David to concentrate on getting well! I'll work with him on catching up when he's feeling better.

The cards on pages 82 and 83 will be a happy surprise for your "under the weather" students. Have classmates sign the inside of the card then mail or send home with a friend.

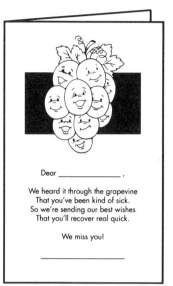

Thank You Notes

Acknowledge the help and support you get from parents by sending home thank you notes. Each Friday spend a few minutes looking back on the week. Jot down the names of parents who made that special effort you appreciate and send home a note to each.

Cheer Up!

Dear _____,

Hope when you receive this letter,
You'll be feeling a little better.
Sit back and relax.
Get lots of rest.
So when you're back at school
You'll be at your best.

Get well soon!

- - - - - - <fold here> - - - - - - - - -

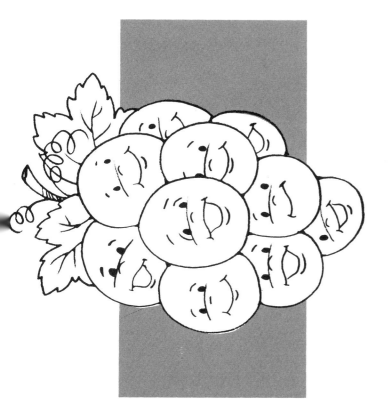

Dear _____,

We heard it through the grapevine
That you've been kind of sick.
So we're sending our best wishes
That you'll recover real quick.

We miss you!

_____

THANK YOU!

<fold here>

I'm so glad
I can count
on you.

Thanks!

Thank You!

Home Visits

Home visits can be a wonderful experience for students, parents and teachers. Call parents at the beginning of the school year and schedule a convenient time that you can meet with the student and the family on their "home turf." Parents feel more relaxed in familiar surroundings, students see home and school as a team working together, and you get a better perspective on a student's life away from school. Use this chart to schedule home visits.

SCHEDULE OF HOME VISITS

Student	Parent's name	Telephone #	Address	Date/time of visit

Parent Communication Activities

Keep parents informed of their children's daily school activities–and you'll get them involved. Journals, "special delivery" folders, newsletters and newspapers are excellent ways to keep families posted not only of special events, but of those important daily activities that comprise the bulk of the school year.

The "What Happened in School Today" Journal

Have each student keep a daily journal that goes back and forth between home and school. At the end of each day, students jot down a few sentences telling about the school day. At home, students read the journal entry to the parents. Parents sign the day's entry and the students return the journals to school. Use the weekly journal page on page 80. Place in a folder or looseleaf binder and hand back all entry pages at the end of the year. It's a great keepsake!

"Special Delivery" Envelopes and Folders

The more a parent knows about a child's work at school, the higher the probability you will get the support you need. Give classwork, corrected tests, awards and positive notes a super send-off every Friday in "special delivery" envelopes or folders. The outside of the envelope or folder should include space for parents to sign, indicating that they have looked at the child's work. Parent comment space should also be included. Tape or staple the "special delivery" form on page 81 to the front of a large manilla envelope or file folder.

My Journal

Name   Grade   Week of

Monday
Today, _____

_____

_____

Tuesday
Today, _____

_____

_____

Wednesday
Today, _____

_____

_____

Thursday
Today, _____

_____

_____

Friday
Today, _____

_____

_____

_____

SPECIAL DELIVERY

for the family of _____

This "special delivery" package might contain classwork, homework, a newsletter, an important note, an announcement, an award—just about anything connected to school. It is very important that you look over the enclosed contents, sign the form and return the "special delivery" envelope/folder to class tomorrow. Keep all classwork, awards and other notes. Return only papers that require your signature or input.

Delivery Date	Parent Signature	Comments

Informed Parents Become Interested Parents

Use a variety of "classroom communiques" to update parents on what has happened during the week and what classroom activities and events will be upcoming.

Have your students assist in the writing, production and distribution of the newsletters. Student participation will elevate parent anticipation of these weekly newsletters.

Weekly Classroom Newsletter

A weekly newsletter will go a long way towards building the bridge of parent support. . .and it doesn't need to be a long, drawn out process. Here are a few ideas:
• **Take ten minutes on Thursday afternoon to review your lesson plans for the week.** Jot down information about interesting lessons, activities, or field trips. Always give special recognition to several students–those who celebrated birthdays, received awards, made excellent progress or (especially for elementary children) lost teeth.

• **Every Thursday afternoon have each student write three sentences telling what they did in school that week.** Choose a sentence from each student and write/type these on a blank seasonal newsletter. Each student underlines his/ her own sentence before taking home the newsletter on Friday. Encourage parents and students to read the newsletter aloud. Suggest to parents that they keep all newsletters in a binder.

Get Out the Word with a Monthly Newspaper

Older students will enjoy planning and producing a monthly newspaper. As a class project, choose several column headings that will be included in every issue. Jobs such as reporter, editor, proofreader, graphics, paste up, printer, etc. are rotated each month. Every student should contribute

something to the newspaper's publication each month. On the next page are a variety of mastheads for classroom newspapers. Use the suggested column heads and clip art on page 92 to give your monthly newspaper a real professional look.

Teacher   Room   Grade   Date

Teacher   Room   Grade   Date

Teacher   Room   Grade   Date

Teacher   Room   Grade   Date

Teacher   Room   Grade   Date

Classroom Newspaper
Column Headings and Clip Art

HOW TO USE:
Reproduce this sheet of paper. Cut out column headlines and/or clip art you will need for this issue of the newspaper. The width of your column will depend on the length of the headline. Use a glue stick or paper cement to paste up all art work. If you are using photographs, use only photocopies of prints.

HAPPENINGS

Parents On Your Side - Resource Materials Workbook

Stay on Track by Keeping Track

It's important to keep track of the notes and awards you send home. Consistently sending "good news" to parents of students who have had problems is important in securing their support when additional problems arise. Use this Documentation Sheet to keep track of your positive communication efforts by circling N for note, PC for phone call and O for other.

Positive Communication Documentation Sheet

N = Note   PC = Phone Call   O = Other

Student	Month of	Month of	Month of	Month of	Month of	Month of
	N PC O	N PC O	N PC O	N PC O	N PC O	N PC O
	N PC O	N PC O	N PC O	N PC O	N PC O	N PC O
	N PC O	N PC O	N PC O	N PC O	N PC O	N PC O
	N PC O	N PC O	N PC O	N PC O	N PC O	N PC O
	N PC O	N PC O	N PC O	N PC O	N PC O	N PC O
	N PC O	N PC O	N PC O	N PC O	N PC O	N PC O
	N PC O	N PC O	N PC O	N PC O	N PC O	N PC O
	N PC O	N PC O	N PC O	N PC O	N PC O	N PC O
	N PC O	N PC O	N PC O	N PC O	N PC O	N PC O
	N PC O	N PC O	N PC O	N PC O	N PC O	N PC O
	N PC O	N PC O	N PC O	N PC O	N PC O	N PC O
	N PC O	N PC O	N PC O	N PC O	N PC O	N PC O
	N PC O	N PC O	N PC O	N PC O	N PC O	N PC O
	N PC O	N PC O	N PC O	N PC O	N PC O	N PC O
	N PC O	N PC O	N PC O	N PC O	N PC O	N PC O
	N PC O	N PC O	N PC O	N PC O	N PC O	N PC O
	N PC O	N PC O	N PC O	N PC O	N PC O	N PC O
	N PC O	N PC O	N PC O	N PC O	N PC O	N PC O
	N PC O	N PC O	N PC O	N PC O	N PC O	N PC O

Involving Parents in the Homework Process Throughout the Year

Homework has the potential to be the most consistent day-to-day contact you can have with parents. Make that contact positive by involving parents in the homework process from the first week of school throughout the entire year. Parents are important to the success of any homework program, not so much for the help they give, but for their motivational and follow-up assistance.

(On page 26 you learned about the importance of developing a homework policy. The policy establishes a foundation for homework by stating your expectations for students, parents and yourself. Your homework program will not be successful unless you follow through all year long by keeping parents informed about classwork, upcoming tests and projects, and ways in which they can help their children study more successfully.

Helpful Homework Hints for Parents

Encourage parents to help their children do a better job on homework by providing them with useful homework and study skills tips. The homework hint sheets on pages 95 and 96 will help children develop good homework habits. Send this home at the beginning of the year so that parents can start immediately helping to improve their child's homework performance.

Helpful Homework Hints for Parents and Students

Homework Hint #1

Choose a well lit, quiet place at home to do homework. Even if most homework is completed at another location after school, there still should be a place in the home in which to study. The kitchen table or a corner of the living room is fine, as long as it is well lit and quiet during homework time.

• Important: Keep the radio and TV off while homework is being done.

• Important: Whenever possible, keep the study area off limits to brothers and sisters during homework time.

Homework Hint #2

Put together a kit that contains the materials usually needed to complete homework assignments. Here is a list of supplies most often required. Grade level recommendations are noted in parentheses. Look through the list and check off the items you will need.

• crayons (1-6)
• pencils (1-12)
• writing paper (1-12)
• markers (1-12)
• pencil sharpener (1-12)
• pens (4-12)
• glue stick, glue or paste (1-12)
• erasers (1-12)
• tape (1-12)
• construction paper (1-12)
• hole punch (4-12)
• stapler (4-12)
• scissors (1-12)
• children's dictionary (1-3)
• paper clips (4-12)
• white out (4-12)
• assignment book (3-12)
• atlas (6-12)
• intermediate dictionary (4-12)
• colored pencils (4-12)
• index cards (5-12)
• folders for reports (4-12)
• thesaurus (7-12)
• almanac (7-12)

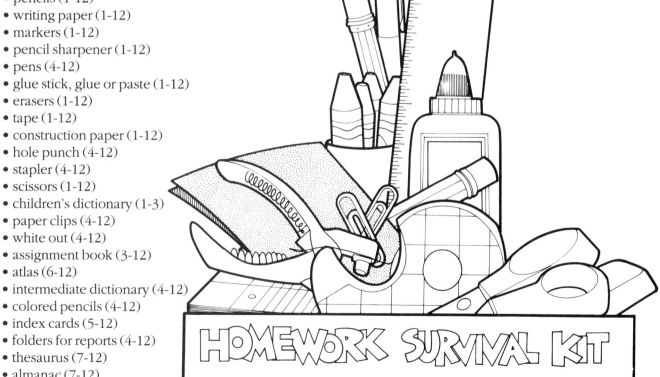

Homework Hint #3

Schedule a specific time each day for homework. For young children the best time is often as soon as they (and the parent) arrive home at the end of the day. Post the schedule on the refrigerator. Both child and parent should initial the chart each day after homework is completed.

Homework Hint #4

By encouraging children to work on their own, a parent helps develop important life skills such as following directions, beginning and completing a task, and time management. Do this every day:

1. Check to see if your child has a homework assignment.

2. Remind your child when homework time has been scheduled.

3. Check to see that your child has all the necessary materials.

4. Ask your child to tell you what the homework assignment is.

5. If necessary, read the directions together with your child. Make sure he or she understands what is expected.

6. For children in grades 4-12, suggest that they call a friend if they need help.

7. Give your child help only if he or she makes a real effort to do the work first.

Homework Hint #5

Children need encouragement and support from the people whose opinions they value the most–their parents. Your consistent praise can encourage your child to feel good about his or her ability and motivate your child to do his or her best work. Don't save your praise only for an "A" on a test. Praise your child efforts made each day. It is, after all, the day-to-day efforts that will lead to higher achievement in school.

Homework and the Home-School Connection

Consistent communication with parents is important in connection with homework. Keeping parents informed of their children's successes and problems with homework is essential. Teachers and parents working together can motivate students to do their best work and help students solve many homework problems. Here are some ideas to keep the home-school connection working effectively throughout the year:

• Create a homework hotline memo.
• Send personalized, positive messages about homework to parents and students.
• Inform and update students and parents about upcoming tests.
• Encourage students to keep track of their homework assignments.

Create a Parent-Teacher Homework Hotline Memo

Initiated by either parent or teacher, this memo/reply form (see page 99) keeps both parties informed about any homework problems or questions. Send home several "homework hotline" memos at the beginning of the year for parents to use when they have any homework concerns.

Positive Homework Notes for Parents

Send home these notes (page 100) when you want to deliver a positive message about homework. These are especially effective if they relate to an assignment the parent has been involved with ("Thanks so much for helping Cindy get the library books she needed,") or if a specific homework problem has been solved ("After doing all his homework for the past two weeks, Jimmy got an 'A' on his math test today. Homework does make a difference.")

Positive Homework Notes for Students

Students, especially those who have improved their homework habits, need special attention for their efforts. Be specific, and generous, with your praise. ("Thank you for writing so neatly. Now your stories are even more fun to read!") See page 101 for student-oriented positive homework notes.

Test Reminder Slips

Give your students, and their parents, ample notice of upcoming tests. Send home test reminder slips (see page 102) several days or weeks before test day.

Keeping Track of Homework Assignments

Put an end to, ". . .but I forgot what the assignment was!" Weekly assignment sheets (see pages 103-104) help ensure that students write down all homework and that parents have an opportunity to see what those assignments are. Staple a weekly assignment sheet to the front of a construction paper folder. Each day students record their homework assignments on the sheets. Work papers are placed in the folder to take home. There's even a parent signature space for parents to sign, indicating that homework assignments have been completed. For secondary students, hole-punch assignment sheets and suggest students keep them in a 3-ring binder.

PARENT - TEACHER
Homework Hotline!

MESSAGE

To: _____ Date _____

_____

_____

_____

_____

_____

_____

From: _____

REPLY

To: _____ Date _____

_____

_____

_____

_____

_____

From: _____

Homework Happy Gram!

It gives me great pleasure to report to you

that _____ has

Student's name

_____

_____

_____

Thanks for your support!

_____

Teacher's name

- -

Homework Happy Gram!

Dear _____ ,

Parent's name

Thought you'd like to know that _____

Student's name

is doing a **SUPER** job on homework because_____

_____

_____

Thanks for your support!

_____

Teacher's name

YOUR HOMEWORK HABITS ARE ROLLIN' RIGHT ALONG!

Dear _____ ,

_____

_____

_____

_____

Thanks, _____ Date _____

Hoppin' Good Homework News!

Dear _____ ,

_____

_____

_____

_____

Thanks, _____ Date _____

Test Time!

Time to start studying for your test.

When: _____

Subject: _____

Place on a bulletin board or your refrigerator to remind you of the test day. Cut off the test reminder at the bottom and return the signed slip to school tomorrow.

☐ I've got a test coming up!

_____
Student's signature

_____
Parent's signature

Test Time!

Time to start studying for your test.

When: _____

Subject: _____

Place on a bulletin board or your refrigerator to remind you of the test day. Cut off the test reminder at the bottom and return the signed slip to school tomorrow.

☐ I've got a test coming up!

_____
Student's signature

_____
Parent's signature

Testing 1-2-3!

We've got a date on: _____

for a TEST in: _____

Better start getting ready now. Post this reminder at home. Return the signed portion below to school tomorrow.

_____
Student's signature

_____
Parent's signature

Testing 1-2-3!

We've got a date on: _____

for a TEST in: _____

Better start getting ready now. Post this reminder at home. Return the signed portion below to school tomorrow.

_____
Student's signature

_____
Parent's signature

Daily Homework Sheet!

Week of _____

MY HOMEWORK FOR MONDAY,

SUBJECT: _____ _____

SUBJECT: _____ _____

SUBJECT: _____ _____

SUBJECT: _____ _____

SUBJECT: _____ _____

MY HOMEWORK FOR TUESDAY,

SUBJECT: _____ _____

SUBJECT: _____ _____

SUBJECT: _____ _____

SUBJECT: _____ _____

SUBJECT: _____ _____

MY HOMEWORK FOR WEDNESDAY,

SUBJECT: _____ _____

SUBJECT: _____ _____

SUBJECT: _____ _____

SUBJECT: _____ _____

SUBJECT: _____ _____

MY HOMEWORK FOR THURSDAY,

SUBJECT: _____ _____

SUBJECT: _____ _____

SUBJECT: _____ _____

SUBJECT: _____ _____

SUBJECT: _____ _____

MY HOMEWORK FOR FRIDAY,

SUBJECT: _____ _____

SUBJECT: _____ _____

SUBJECT: _____ _____

SUBJECT: _____ _____

SUBJECT: _____ _____

TESTS THIS WEEK

SUBJECT:_____ SUBJECT:_____

SUBJECT:_____ SUBJECT:_____

SUBJECT:_____ SUBJECT:_____

HOMEWORK ASSIGNMENT SHEET

Week of _____

MONDAY

SUBJECT: _____ _____

SUBJECT: _____ _____

SUBJECT: _____ _____

SUBJECT: _____ _____

SUBJECT: _____ _____

SUBJECT: _____ _____

TUESDAY

SUBJECT: _____ _____

SUBJECT: _____ _____

SUBJECT: _____ _____

SUBJECT: _____ _____

SUBJECT: _____ _____

SUBJECT: _____ _____

WEDNESDAY

SUBJECT: _____ _____

SUBJECT: _____ _____

SUBJECT: _____ _____

SUBJECT: _____ _____

SUBJECT: _____ _____

SUBJECT: _____ _____

THURSDAY

SUBJECT: _____ _____

SUBJECT: _____ _____

SUBJECT: _____ _____

SUBJECT: _____ _____

SUBJECT: _____ _____

SUBJECT: _____ _____

FRIDAY

SUBJECT: _____ _____

SUBJECT: _____ _____

SUBJECT: _____ _____

SUBJECT: _____ _____

SUBJECT: _____ _____

SUBJECT: _____ _____

TESTS OR REPORTS THIS WEEK

SUBJECT: _____ _____

SUBJECT: _____ _____

SUBJECT: _____ _____

SUBJECT: _____ _____

SUBJECT: _____ _____

SUBJECT: _____ _____

Document All Problems

Documentation of a child's misbehavior or classroom problems (academic, behavior, or social) is imperative when dealing with parents. Documentation strengthens your position as a professional and communicates clearly to parents that these problems do exist.

Start documenting problems at the beginning of the school year.

It is very important to begin writing anecdotal records as soon as problems begin surfacing, especially when you seek the support of administrators and parents. No matter what method of documentation you use, remember:

• **Be specific.** Keep away from vague opinions. Your statements should be based on factual, observable data:

> *"Yesterday Chris threw his lunch tray on the ground and shoved other children In three separate instances."*

> *"Today during reading, Marcia repeatedly jumped up and bothered the students around her."*
> *"For the third day in a row, John has failed to bring either his algebra book or his homework to class."*

• **Be consistent.** Document problems each time they occur. Repeated occurrences may show a pattern and be helpful in solving the problem.

Documenting problems on a monthly log sheet.

Reproduce a Behavior Documentation Sheet (page 107) at the beginning of each month. Place it in a file folder on your desk. When a student chooses not to follow classroom rules, write his or her name on the sheet and document the problem and your action taken.

Documenting problems on individual pages in a 3-ring binder.

Many educators keep individual documentation sheets on each student in their classroom. A spiral-bound notebook or a looseleaf binder (see page 108) with a separate page designated for each student works well.

Documenting problems on cards in a file box.

Some teachers use the file-box technique. Each student is assigned a separate 3x5 index card. These cards are arranged alphabetically in the file box. Reproduce the cards on page 109, one for each student. Consider duplicating the cards on index stock for added durability. Fold in half with name facing forward.

Keep track of daily infractions with a plan book insert.

Use the plan book insert on page 110 to keep an accurate count of students who choose not to follow your classroom rules. Write each student's name (in alphabetical order) on the insert. If a student receives a warning, circle the word "warning" on the chart next to his or her name. If the student continues to misbehave, circle the corresponding number of the consequence. Start new each morning. One insert will last you the entire week. At the end of the week, either transfer the information to individual student sheets or place the insert in a binder.

Whatever method of documentation you choose, you need to keep it in a convenient place so that you can record information efficiently during the school day. It is important to include the following information:

• student's name
• date, time and place of incident
• description of the problem
• action taken
• (Optional) phone number where parents can be reached

Behavior Documentation Sheet

Month of _____

Student Name	Date/Time	Place	Behavior	Disciplinary Action Taken

Individual Behavior Documentation Sheet

STUDENT NAME _____

Parent(s) Name(s) _____

Home Phone # _____ Work Phone # _____

Address _____

•**Date** _____ Time _____ Place _____

Description of Problem/Incident: _____

_____

Action Taken: _____

_____

•**Date** _____ Time _____ Place _____

Description of Problem/Incident: _____

_____

Action Taken: _____

_____

•**Date** _____ Time _____ Place _____

Description of Problem/Incident: _____

_____

Action Taken: _____

_____

•**Date** _____ Time _____ Place _____

Description of Problem/Incident: _____

_____

Action Taken: _____

_____

•**Date** _____ Time _____ Place _____

Description of Problem/Incident: _____

_____

Action Taken: _____

_____

Student _____ Phone # _____

Parent's Name _____ Work # _____

Parent's Name _____ Work # _____

•**Date** _____ Time _____ Place _____

Description of Problem/Incident: _____

_____

Action Taken: _____

•**Date** _____ Time _____ Place _____

Description of Problem/Incident: _____

Action Taken: _____

•**Date** _____ Time _____ Place _____

Description of Problem/Incident: _____

Action Taken: _____

•**Date** _____ Time _____ Place _____

Description of Problem/Incident: _____

Action Taken: _____

< fold here >

Student _____ Phone # _____

Parent's Name _____ Work # _____

Parent's Name _____ Work # _____

•**Date** _____ Time _____ Place _____

Description of Problem/Incident: _____

_____

Action Taken: _____

•**Date** _____ Time _____ Place _____

Description of Problem/Incident: _____

Action Taken: _____

•**Date** _____ Time _____ Place _____

Description of Problem/Incident: _____

Action Taken: _____

•**Date** _____ Time _____ Place _____

Description of Problem/Incident: _____

Action Taken: _____

BEHAVIOR TRACKING SHEET

WEEK OF _____

Name	MONDAY	TUESDAY	WEDNESDAY	THURSDAY	FRIDAY
	Warning 2 3 4 5	Warning 2 3 4 5	Warning 2 3 4 5	Warning 2 3 4 5	Warning 2 3 4 5
	Warning 2 3 4 5	Warning 2 3 4 5	Warning 2 3 4 5	Warning 2 3 4 5	Warning 2 3 4 5
	Warning 2 3 4 5	Warning 2 3 4 5	Warning 2 3 4 5	Warning 2 3 4 5	Warning 2 3 4 5
	Warning 2 3 4 5	Warning 2 3 4 5	Warning 2 3 4 5	Warning 2 3 4 5	Warning 2 3 4 5
	Warning 2 3 4 5	Warning 2 3 4 5	Warning 2 3 4 5	Warning 2 3 4 5	Warning 2 3 4 5
	Warning 2 3 4 5	Warning 2 3 4 5	Warning 2 3 4 5	Warning 2 3 4 5	Warning 2 3 4 5
	Warning 2 3 4 5	Warning 2 3 4 5	Warning 2 3 4 5	Warning 2 3 4 5	Warning 2 3 4 5
	Warning 2 3 4 5	Warning 2 3 4 5	Warning 2 3 4 5	Warning 2 3 4 5	Warning 2 3 4 5
	Warning 2 3 4 5	Warning 2 3 4 5	Warning 2 3 4 5	Warning 2 3 4 5	Warning 2 3 4 5
	Warning 2 3 4 5	Warning 2 3 4 5	Warning 2 3 4 5	Warning 2 3 4 5	Warning 2 3 4 5
	Warning 2 3 4 5	Warning 2 3 4 5	Warning 2 3 4 5	Warning 2 3 4 5	Warning 2 3 4 5
	Warning 2 3 4 5	Warning 2 3 4 5	Warning 2 3 4 5	Warning 2 3 4 5	Warning 2 3 4 5
	Warning 2 3 4 5	Warning 2 3 4 5	Warning 2 3 4 5	Warning 2 3 4 5	Warning 2 3 4 5
	Warning 2 3 4 5	Warning 2 3 4 5	Warning 2 3 4 5	Warning 2 3 4 5	Warning 2 3 4 5
	Warning 2 3 4 5	Warning 2 3 4 5	Warning 2 3 4 5	Warning 2 3 4 5	Warning 2 3 4 5
	Warning 2 3 4 5	Warning 2 3 4 5	Warning 2 3 4 5	Warning 2 3 4 5	Warning 2 3 4 5
	Warning 2 3 4 5	Warning 2 3 4 5	Warning 2 3 4 5	Warning 2 3 4 5	Warning 2 3 4 5

To the teacher: When a student receives a warning, write the student's name on this tracking sheet. If a student breaks additional rules during that school day, circle each consequence on the appropriate box. For example, if a student receives a warning and chooses not to follow the rules again during the day, you would record   Warning (2) (3) 4 5.

Contact Parents When Problems Arise

When should a teacher contact a parent? Get in touch with parents at the first sign of a problem that could escalate into something more troublesome. It doesn't matter if it's the first week of school or the first day of school. If you want parent support, you must let them know what's happening–all the time.

Use the Telephone to Contact Parents

The most effective communication tool for contacting parents when there is an issue that needs prompt attention is the telephone. It gives you instant access to parents.

A telephone call can be effective only if you are fully prepared. Planning is the key to a productive call. Jot down what you plan to say before you dial (use the Parent Phone Call Worksheet on page 112). After the phone call, file this sheet with your other documentation records.

Follow these guidelines:

Start with a statement of concern.

> *"Mrs. Jones, I'm calling because I'm concerned about how little work Jared is getting done in class."*

Describe the specific behavior that necessitated the call.

> *"The reason I'm concerned is Jared has refused to do any of his work in class for two days now."*

Describe the steps you have taken to solve the problem.

> *"When Jared refused to do his work, I had him stay in my room during lunch to complete his assignments. I have spoken with him on three occasions regarding how he needs to complete his work."*

Get parental input.

> *"Is there anything you can tell me that might help us solve this problem?"*

Present your solution to the problem.

> *"Here's what I will do at school: I'll continue to give Jared plenty of positive reinforcement when he does do his work. When he doesn't, he will stay in at recess or lunch to complete it. But most important, here's what I'd like you to do: Please tell Jared that I called, and that I am concerned that he is not doing his work. Tell him that you are concerned, too. I want Jared to know that both of us are working together to help him do better in school."*

Express confidence in your ability to solve the problem.

> *"Mrs. Jones, I've worked with many children like your Jared. Don't worry. Together we will help him."*

Inform parents that there will be follow-up contact from you.

> *"I will contact you in two days and let you know how things are going."*

Use the phone call worksheet on page 113 to guide you through a call if the problem has not improved.

PARENT PHONE CALL WORKSHEET
Guidelines for an INITIAL PHONE CALL about a problem

Teacher _____ Grade _____ Date of call _____

Student _____

Parent or Guardian _____

Home phone # _____ Work phone # _____

Write down important points you will cover in this call:

1. Begin with a statement of concern. _____

_____

2. Describe the specific behavior that necessitated your call. _____

_____

_____

3. Describe the steps you have taken to solve the problem. _____

_____

_____

4. Get parent input. _____

_____

_____

5. Record parent comments. _____

_____

6. Present your solutions to the problem. _____

_____

   What you will do: _____

_____

   What you want the parent to do: _____

_____

7. Express confidence in your ability to solve the problem. _____

_____

8. Tell parents that there will be follow-up contact from you. _____

_____

Notes: _____

_____

_____

PARENT PHONE CALL WORKSHEET

Guidelines for FOLLOW-UP CONTACT if a problem has not improved

Teacher _____ Grade _____ Date of call _____

Student _____

Parent or Guardian _____

Home phone # _____ Work phone # _____

In the spaces below, write down important points you will cover with the parents.

1. Begin with a statement of concern. _____

_____

2. Describe the problem behavior (state in observable terms). _____

_____

_____

3. Review what you have done to solve the problem. _____

_____

_____

4. Get parent input. _____

_____

5. Record parent comments. _____

_____

_____

6. Present your solutions to the problem. _____

    What you will do: _____

_____

    What you want the parent to do: _____

_____

7. Express confidence once again in your ability to solve the problem. _____

_____

_____

Notes: _____

_____

_____

Contacting Hard-to-Reach Parents

Send a letter when you are unable to reach a parent by phone. Use school stationery if possible, or use the "Urgent" letterhead on page 115. All letters should be mailed, not sent with the student. Address the same details you would have discussed in a phone call:

1. Show your concern for the student.

2. State the specific problem the student is having.

3. List the steps you have taken to help the student with the problem.

4. Explain exactly what you would like the parent to do.

5. Let the parent know that you are confident that, by working together, the problem will be solved.

6. Ask the parent to contact you immediately by phone or note.

If you are unable to reach a parent by phone or note, don't give up.

If necessary:
- Call the parent at work.
- Call the student's emergency number and leave a message.
- Send a registered letter or mailgram.

URGENT

URGENT

AN URGENT MESSAGE FROM SCHOOL
Please read and respond as soon as possible.

_____
_____
_____
_____
_____
_____
_____
_____
_____
_____
_____
_____
_____
_____
_____
_____
_____
_____
_____
_____
_____

How to Conduct a Problem-Solving Parent Conference

When a phone call or note to a parent doesn't solve a problem, or if a specific problem seems to warrant it, you will need to meet in a face-to-face conference with the parent. A problem-solving conference gives both teacher and parent the opportunity to get information and give input that might help solve the current "crisis." Follow these steps when planning a problem-solving conference:

Step #1

Decide who will be involved in the conference. Decide whether or not the student should be present. If the student's presence makes the parent uncomfortable, or if the child is disruptive, don't do it. But if you need input from the student, involve him or her in part of the conference. The best reason for having a student there is to demonstrate the solidarity of teacher and parent in wanting to work together to help the student.

Step #2

Plan what you will say to the parent. Plan a friendly, positive atmosphere. Before you meet, write down the important points you want to cover with the parent. When preparing, ask yourself, "How would I feel if I were the parent in this situation? How would I want the teacher to treat me?" Then let that awareness guide your words and actions. Use the Conference Planning Sheet on page 117 to help you organize your comments.

Step #3

Gather documentation. Parents often need to see proof that a problem does exist. Make sure you have all of your documentation with you at the conference. Put it in chronological order to give a clear picture of how the problem has progressed.

Problem-Solving Conference

Planning Sheet

Teacher _____ Grade _____ Date of conference _____

Student _____ Parent or Guardian _____

1. Begin with a statement of concern, updating the situation. _____
   _____

2. Describe the specific problem and present documentation. _____
   _____

3. Describe what you have already done to solve the problem. _____
   _____

4. Get parental input on the problem. _____
   Remarks: _____
   _____

5. Get parental input on how to solve the problem. _____
   Remarks: _____
   _____

6. Tell the parent what you will do to help solve the problem. _____
   _____

7. Explain what you need the parent to do to solve the problem. _____
   _____

8. Let the parent know that you are confident that the problem can be worked out.

9. Tell the parent that there will be follow-up contact from you. _____
   _____

10. Review the conference. _____
    _____
    _____

Notes: _____
   _____
   _____

Involving Parents in Problem Solving

After conferencing with a parent, how do you ensure success for the goals you have set? How can you make certain you get the support you need? The best way to successfully ensure a parent's effort is by using a home-school contract.

What is a home-school contract?

A home-school contract is a written agreement between teacher, student and parent. The contract states that the student agrees to a specific behavior. If the student complies with the terms of the agreement, he or she will earn special rewards–praise, privileges and small prizes.

When should a home-school contract be used?

Use this technique to correct behavior problems in school and academic problems with classwork or homework. A contract is warranted when you can answer "yes" to any of these questions:
• Could the student benefit from a structured system of positive and negative consequences?

• Does the parent need daily feedback regarding the student's behavior at school?
• Have you tried to solve the problem through other means, without success?
• Do you suspect that the student receives little positive reinforcement at home?
• Has a student's parent asked for help from you in solving a student's problem?

How to Write and Present a Successful Home-School Contract

The home-school contract is a team effort between teacher and parent. Present the contract (page 120) as part of a problem-solving conference. Follow these steps:

Step #1–Introduce the concept of the home-school contract to the parent.
A detailed explanation is very important. Explain the reason for using the contract and the elements that will determine its success. Stress consistency, the use of praise and follow-through with consequences when the child chooses not to follow the terms of the contract.

Step #2–Determine how you want the student to behave.
Fill in the desired behavior on the contract.

Step #3–Explain the positive consequences you will give the student for appropriate behavior.
When the student chooses to behave, you will reinforce this behavior with a variety of positive actions at school. Spell them out for the parent: first in line, class monitor, free reading time, stickers, award certificate, healthy snacks, etc. Junior high and high school students need positives that are appropriate for their grade: homework

privilege pass, coupon for campus "snack shack", positive postcard sent to parents, etc. When you have decided upon the appropriate positive, fill in the contract.

Step #4–Help the parent choose positive consequences to be used at home.

When the child behaves at school, he or she must be rewarded at home, too. Parent praise and support is vital to the success of this program. Brainstorm ideas for positive consequences the parent can provide at home: staying up late one night, renting a favorite video, choosing dessert, buying a new book, etc. Fill in the contract.

Step #5–Explain the negative consequence you will provide if the student chooses not to comply.

Every time a student does not comply with the contract, a negative consequence will be imposed: stay after school 15 minutes, a note sent home explaining the student's behavior, etc. Fill in the contract.

Step #6–Help the parent choose negative consequences to be used at home.

When the child misbehaves at school, he or she must receive negative consequences at home, too. This is difficult for some parents, but stress that consistency is the key to solving the problem. When a child misbehaves at school, the parent will: take away TV, radio or telephone privileges, restrict use of bike (or car for older children) or other sports equipment, ground child for a day (or weekend, depending on child's age), etc. Fill in the contract.

Step #7–Decide on the duration of the contract.

How long will the terms of the contract be in effect: a week, two weeks, a month? Consider the child's age and the problem when deciding. Usually, the younger the child, the shorter the duration of the contract should be. Remember, your goal is for the child to succeed. Don't doom the contract to failure before you begin by making the expectations too unreachable. Fill in the contract.

Step #8–Sign and present the contract.

The home-school contract must be signed by all involved parties–student, teacher and parent. When having the student sign, show a warm and positive attitude that says, "This is an opportunity for things to change for the better. This is not a punishment."

Daily Parent Contact Is Essential for Home-School Contract Success

Each day the contract is in effect, you must send home a note letting the parent know how the student behaved in class that day. Your note should include: the date, how the student behaved, action you took (positive reinforcement or negative consequences, and what the parent needs to do at home. Use the daily contact sheets on page 121.

Home-School Contract

(Student's name) _____

promises to:(describe desired behavior) _____

_____

_____

☐ **Each day the student does as agreed, he/she can expect the following positive reinforcement:**

From the teacher:

1. _____

2. _____

3. _____

From the parent:

1. _____

2. _____

☐ **Each day the student does not do as agreed, he/she can expect the following negative consequence:**

From the teacher:

1. _____

2. _____

From the parent:

1. _____

2. _____

This contract will be in effect from _____ to _____ .

Student signature _____

Parent signature _____

Teacher signature _____

Home-School Contract
Daily Contact Sheet

Student's name _____ Date _____

Dear _____,

___ Today your child behaved according to the terms of the contract. I have given the positive reinforcement that we agreed upon. Please follow through at home with your positive reinforcement, also.

___ Today your child did **not** behave according to the terms of the contract. I have given the negative consequences that we agreed upon. Please follow through at home with your negative consequences, also.

Please get in touch with me if you have any questions or if you would like to talk about the contract.

Sincerely, _____

Additional comments: _____

_____

_____

_____

- -

Home-School Contract
Daily Contact Sheet

Student's name _____ Date _____

Dear _____,

___ Today your child behaved according to the terms of the contract. I have given the positive reinforcement that we agreed upon. Please follow through at home with your positive reinforcement, also.

___ Today your child did **not** behave according to the terms of the contract. I have given the negative consequences that we agreed upon. Please follow through at home with your negative consequences, also.

Please get in touch with me if you have any questions or if you would like to talk about the contract.

Sincerely, _____

Additional comments: _____

_____

_____

_____

How to Conduct a Parent Conference that Builds Parent Support

You have several built-in opportunities a year to build parent support–at parent conferences. A regularly scheduled conference can be a pleasant, informative and productive meeting for both parent and teacher. If you use the conference arena to get to know one another and to interact on behalf of the student, you'll have a classroom of parents on your side. The success of the regularly scheduled conference, however, rests in your hands in the thoroughness of your preparation and the professional, comfortable way you conduct the conference.

Send home a conference invitation.

The invitation you send home should be warm, friendly and informative (see page 123) and it should include the following information:

1. The purpose of this parent conference.

Specify why the conference is planned. If your reasons are too vague some parents may not come, thinking they might hear only bad news about their child or that the conference will be an unnecessary waste of their time. Inform them that all parents will be attending conferences and that they are extremely important.

2. Offer parents flexible time choices.

In this day of single parents and two-income families, you must offer conferences times that fit into your parents' busy schedules.

On the invitation give parents as much choice as possible in choosing the day of the week and time of their conference.

3. Ask for parent input about what they would like to discuss.

Include a section for the parent to list any issues he or she would like to discuss at the conference. This gives you an opportunity to think in advance about the issues and be better prepared to give input or answers.

4. Write a personal comment on the invitation.

By personalizing a reproduced letter, you are showing parents that you've put in a bit more effort and care. Jot down a friendly "I'm looking forward to talking with you" at the bottom of the invitation. And be sure to sign your name.

Send home conference reminder notices for maximum attendance.

As you receive confirmation from each parent, fill out a conference reminder notice and place it in your plan book. Send home a reminder to each parent a day or two before their scheduled conference. Use the reminder notices on page 124.

You're Invited!

To the parents of _____ ,

During the week of _____, I will be holding parent-teacher conferences. I look forward to talking with you about your child's education this year. We have an important job to do–to make this a productive, happy year for your child. At the conference we will discuss your child's progress, my goals for the year, and any other issues that effect your child. I am certain working together, we can make this the best year ever for your child.

I have scheduled your parent conference for (day) _____,

(date) _____ at (time) _____

Please fill out the R.S.V.P. portion of this invitation and send it back to school. If you have any questions you'd like to discuss with me at the conference, please write them on the R.S.V.P. form. It's important that we have the opportunity to talk about issues that are important to you.

Sincerely,

- -

R.S.V.P.

___   Yes, I can attend the parent conference at the scheduled time.

___   No, I can't make the scheduled time. If possible, please reschedule me for

(day) _____, (date) _____, (time) _____

I would like to discuss these concerns at parent conference: _____

_____

_____

(Parent) _____ (Student's name) _____

Confirmation

Dear Parent,

I have rescheduled your parent conference for (day) _____,

(date) _____, (time) _____

Please contact me if this is inconvenient.

_____

Teacher's signature

Dear _____ ,

Our parent conference is scheduled for tomorrow,

(date) _____ , at

(time) _____ .

 I look forward to talking with you.

Sincerely,

Dear _____ ,

Our parent conference is scheduled for tomorrow,

(date) _____ , at

(time) _____ .

 I look forward to talking with you.

Sincerely,

Dear _____ ,

Our parent conference is scheduled for tomorrow,

(date) _____ , at

(time) _____ .

 I look forward to talking with you.

Sincerely,

Dear _____ ,

Our parent conference is scheduled for tomorrow,

(date) _____ , at

(time) _____ .

 I look forward to talking with you.

Sincerely,

Set the stage for a successful conference.

The Conference Setting

It's very important that parents are comfortable during the conference. Arrange to have adult-sized chairs in your room during the conference. If possible, set up a coffee maker and offer coffee and/or tea. Don't forget to place two chairs outside the door for early arrivals. Your door should be clearly labeled with your name and room number. (See page 126 for door poster.)

The Student Sampler

Have examples of a student's classwork available for the conference. Use the work to help you illustrate statements you are making to parents regarding their child's performance in class. Place the work in a construction paper folder. (See page 127 for cover sheet.)

The Parent Conference Form

Because you have a limited amount of time, your conference must be tightly scheduled. Write down all the issues you wish to discuss with a parent. Use the parent conference sheet on page 128 to help you plan your conference. Here are several points that should be addressed with parents at the conference:

1. Begin by sharing an example of the unique qualities of their child.

2. Give an update on any past problems.

3. Discuss academic strengths.

4. If appropriate, discuss academic weaknesses.

5. Get parental input on the child's academic performance.

6. Discuss academic goals for the remainder of the year.

7. Present the social strengths of the student.

8. If appropriate, discuss the student's weaknesses in social interactions.

9. Discuss your goals in the area of social development for the remainder of the year.

10. Get parental input regarding their child's social behavior.

Welcome

to Parent Conference.
Please have a seat
I'll be with you
very soon.

_____
Teacher's Name

_____
Room #

A Sample of Your Child's Classwork

_____

Student's Name

_____

Teacher's Name   Room #

PARENT CONFERENCE
PLANNING AND NOTE SHEET

Student's name _____ Conference date _____

Parent(s) name(s) _____ Time _____

1. Example of student's unique quality. _____
    _____

2. Past problems to be updated at the conference._____
    _____

3. Academic strengths of the student. _____
    _____

4. If appropriate, areas of academic weakness. _____
    _____

5. Academic goals for the student for the rest of the year. _____
    _____

6. Parent input on student academic performance. Parent comments:_____
    _____

7. Social strengths of the student._____
    _____

8. If appropriate, weaknesses in social development. _____
    _____

9. Social development goals for the remainder of the school year. _____
    _____

10. Parent input regarding student's social behavior. Parent comments: _____
    _____

11. Additional issues that parent wishes to discuss. _____
    _____

Additional conference notes: _____
    _____
    _____
    _____